POWER MOVES

What the Bible Says About How You Can Reclaim and Redefine Your God-Given Power

STUDY GUIDE

SARAH JAKES ROBERTS

WITH LAURA SIMPSON

HarperChristian Resources

Power Moves Bible Study Guide
© 2024 by Sarah Jakes Roberts

Published in Grand Rapids, Michigan, by HarperChristian Resources. HarperChristian Resources is a registered trademark of HarperCollins Christian Publishing, Inc.

Requests for information should be sent to customercare@harpercollins.com.

ISBN 978-0-3101-5105-0 (softcover)
ISBN 978-0-3101-5106-7 (ebook)

HarperChristian Resources titles may be purchased in bulk for church, business, fundraising, or ministry use. For information, please e-mail ResourceSpecialist@ ChurchSource.com.

First Printing November 2024 / Printed in the United States of America

CONTENTS

When [Jesus] noticed how the guests picked the places of
honor at the table, he told them this parable:
"When someone invites you to a wedding feast, do not take
the place of honor, for a person more distinguished than you
may have been invited. If so, the host who invited both of you will
come and say to you, 'Give this person your seat.'
Then, humiliated, you will have to take the least important place.
But when you are invited, take the lowest place, so that
when your host comes, he will say to you, 'Friend, move up
to a better place.' Then you will be honored in the presence of all
the other guests. For all those who exalt themselves will be humbled,
and those who humble themselves will be exalted."

LUKE 14:7–11

A NOTE FROM
Sarah Jakes Roberts

One of the earliest definitions of *power* dates to the thirteenth century. It is defined in the *Oxford English Dictionary* as the "ability to act or affect something strongly."[1] If you have ever found yourself withdrawing or isolating because you're confused, doubtful, or nervous, it's not because you are weak. It's evidence that your power—your ability to affect something strongly—is under attack. For most of us, it was taken before we realized how precious it was. When we experience distress, it doesn't just wound us; it robs us. It drains us of power before we can even patch the hole.

You might be able to acknowledge that you have been changed by that theft. You may agree that you have been drained of your power. But did you know that you don't have to accept this inwardly frustrated state you're in? The reclamation of your power is an act of defiance. Your days of faking it until you make it are over. Your power *can* be restored.

My life has been marked by evidence of this truth. My relationship with God has awakened me to more than just a life of penance and remorse. I have discovered that dry bones can live again, joy does come in the morning, and abundant life exists after heartbreak. In this Bible study guide, I want to share with you some of what I've learned from Scripture about reclaiming and redefining your God-given power. It is going to be liberating in ways you didn't even realize you needed—and the best part is that it won't require you to pretend.

Even more, I want to show you how you can maintain *staying power* in your life. The *Collins English Dictionary* defines staying power as "the strength or determination to keep going until you reach the end of what you are doing."[2] *Merriam-Webster* says that staying power is the "capacity for continuing (as in existence, influence, or popularity) without weakening."[3] If we merge the two definitions together, it leaves us with this statement to ponder: *Staying power is having the capacity to exercise strength or determination in trusting God without weakening.* Power is not about you at all. It's about living your life as an ode to the Most High.

As you work through this study, my only request is that you be honest with yourself. Know that some of the truths that will surface may not be something you're ready for anyone else to hear. But that's okay. Where you start may not be where you land, but until you learn to make space for your truth, you cannot tap into the fullness of God's goodness concerning your life, nor can you reasonably expect anyone else to do the same.

I am honored to be your guide on this journey of reclamation. As Paul wrote, "I pray that the eyes of your heart may be enlightened in order that you may know the hope to which he has called you, the riches of his glorious inheritance in his holy people, and his incomparably great power for us who believe" (Ephesians 1:18–19). This is my prayer for you as well—that God would use the words of this study to bring you back to power.

— SARAH JAKES ROBERTS

HOW TO USE THIS
Bible Study Guide

Welcome to the *Power Moves* Bible study. This guide is designed to help you understand what it means to have God's power moving in you, through you, and for you so that you can have a positive impact for Him in this world. He has designed you to be a force! Before you begin, there are a few ways you can go through this material. You can experience this study with others in a group (such as a Bible study, Sunday school class, or any other small-group gathering), or you may choose to go through the content on your own. Either way, you will maximize your experience by using it alongside the *Power Moves* book.

The sessions in this guide will provide you with a basic framework on how to open your group time together, get the most out of the content, and discuss some key ideas from the book that you are studying together. Each session includes the following:

- **Big Idea:** The opening box lists what chapters to read in *Power Moves* and provides some of the key ideas that will be covered in the session.

- **Opening Reading:** A short story or illustration about the topic of the session for you to either read on your own or read through together as a group.

- **Opening Prayer:** A short prompt on how to open your group time in prayer.

- **Beginning Question:** An icebreaker question to get you and your group members thinking about the topic and interacting with one another.

- **Consider Your Life:** A short exercise for you to do on your own to help you reflect on your life as it applies to the topic of the session.

- **Discuss as a Group:** Questions to help you and your group "marinate" on the book material, engage in discussion, and apply the concepts to your lives.

- **Apply What You Learned:** A short personal exercise for you to do after the group discussion time to help you activate the message in your life.

- **Pray to Close:** A short prompt on how to close your group time in prayer.

- **Looking Ahead:** A brief note on what will be covered in the next session.

If you are doing this study in a group, have your own copy of this Bible study guide so you can write down your thoughts, responses, and reflections and complete the assessments. You will also want to have your own copy of the *Power Moves* book to read during the week. Finally, keep these points in mind:

- **Facilitation:** You will want to appoint someone to serve as the group facilitator. This person will be responsible for keeping track of the time during discussions and activities and generally making sure things run smoothly. If *you* have been chosen for this role, there are some resources in the back of this guide that can help you lead your group through the study.

- **Faithfulness:** Your small group is a place where growth can happen as you reflect on the Bible, ask questions, and learn what God is doing in one another's lives. For this reason, be fully committed and attend each session so you can build trust and rapport with the other members.

- **Friendship:** The goal of any small group is to serve as a place where people share, learn about God, and build friendships. So seek to make your group a safe place. Be honest about your thoughts and feelings ... but also listen to everyone else's thoughts, feelings, and opinions. Keep anything personal that your group members share in confidence so that you can create a community where people can heal, be challenged, and grow spiritually.

If you are unable to read through all the chapters assigned from *Power Moves* in any given week, please still plan on attending the group time. You will get a lot out of listening to the other group members even if you have not done all the reading, and the group members will still benefit from hearing your insights on the questions. Above all, as you go through this study, listen for what God is saying to you and what He wants you to learn. Be open to hearing what the Bible says about the power that God has made available to you in your life.

Power Through Connection

Read chapters 1–3 in *Power Moves* by Sarah Jakes Roberts.

Big Idea: Maybe you've felt like you've had power "drained" from you and are unable to do anything for God. But He has bigger plans for you than you have for yourself. He will infuse you with power so that you can accomplish His plans through your connection with Him.

Scan to hear a word on this session from Sarah.

"There's no such thing as no access to power. Your breath is evidence that power is still accessible to you. If you have breath, you have access. But until we go within and figure out what's not functioning properly, we can't take advantage of the access to power that we possess. . . . When the power is flowing, it's not much different from water gushing through a water hose at full speed. It moves without restriction. It takes on many different forms without being committed to any particular way of being. When your power is flowing, you have the ability to act or affect something strongly.

— SARAH JAKES ROBERTS [4]

Once upon a time, people had to hold their cell phones toward the ceiling and get near a door or window just to get a bar of signal. We didn't know it at the time, but a power source was soon coming that would provide access at all times: *the wireless network*. It didn't matter if you were in a basement or behind a wall, if you were near the source, you had connection.

When the Wi-Fi signal in your home is strong, you can do most anything on your phone. You can order food, talk to a friend across the world, play games, look up information, and take a picture—all at the same time. But what happens when you back out of your driveway or take a few steps into your backyard? Your podcast starts to skip. Your texts take an extra few seconds to send. The voice on the other end of the call suddenly gets garbled.

Why is this happening? You've moved too far away from the power source for your network. Your phone is probably in the process of switching over to a different source, like data, which (depending on your coverage) might be less reliable and less efficient. As a result, you are experiencing lags in speed and even the dreaded phenomenon known as *buffering*.

The same thing can happen in your life. The Bible is clear that your source of power comes from God. He is your ultimate "wireless network" who provides the guidance and strength you need to operate effectively in life. So it only stands to reason that if you get too far away from this ultimate power source, you will start to feel stuck, slow, and ineffective.

Where are you in proximity to God's network signal? Does it feel as if your goals are taking a lifetime to achieve? Are there plans God has for you that you have put off to the side because your signal with Him is low? Are there disruptions in your connection?

Or maybe the problem is that you are not aware that you have access to God's incredible power source. Back in the garden of Eden, as we will explore in this session, God gave Adam and Eve the authority to subdue the earth and have dominion over it. Yet they allowed the enemy to talk them out of giving up their position and ended up undermining themselves instead of embracing their power. We have lived with the repercussions and consequences ever since. But it's not the way it's supposed to be.

There *is* a different way. You don't have to live as a victim or in the world of "I can't." But it's not an overnight process . . . and will take some work. You will have to let some things *marinate* before you can *activate*. So, as you begin this study, commit to being honest with yourself, with God, and with others. Authenticity is the key here. By examining your power, your values, and your capacity, you are setting out on a road toward reclaiming your God-given power. You are going to work through some tough truths and answer some hard questions, but each session will bring you closer to God and empower you to live the life that He has for you.

OPENING PRAYER

Lord, I am tired of feeling powerless. I know there are areas I need to address head-on. Prepare my heart to hear Your truth and give me patience to learn to walk with You through breakdowns that lead to breakthroughs. As I go through this study, help me to be honest with You and give me eyes to see the work You are doing in my life. In Your name, amen.

BEGINNING QUESTION

If you are doing this study as part of a group, take a moment to introduce yourselves. Then get things started by discussing one of the following questions:

- What do you hope to experience from this study?

  — *or* —

- What comes to mind when you think of God's power?

CONSIDER YOUR LIFE

It's hard to know how much you've grown if you can't recall where you started. So take a moment to do the following assessment on your own. In the table below, first make a list of four areas in your life where you currently feel powerless. This could include situations where you find yourself continually conforming to the opinions of others, or where you feel resentful at other people's ability to express themselves (in a way you can't seem to do), or any other situation where you feel trapped and unable to move ahead.

	Areas where you feel powerless	What would change if you gained power
1		
2		
3		
4		

Now, in the next column, write down how you envision your life would change if you gained power in that area. (For example, "If I didn't continually conform to the opinions of others, I wouldn't find myself doing things that I really didn't want to do in the first place.") At the end of this study, you will return to this assessment to see what has changed and improved in your life.

DISCUSS AS A GROUP

Use these questions to help you engage with what you learned in chapters 1–3 of *Power Moves*. These questions are meant to help you sit and ponder your answer. The best part of a good "marination" is the multiple ingredients that come together to make something flavorful. The same will apply to your group. Don't be afraid to share your answers. When you take the time to soak in the presence of God, you will become a rich nourishment for others.

1. It is important to again state up front that true power in your life comes from *God*. Read Romans 5:6–8. How does Paul describe your condition before Jesus died for you? What does he say about your power and your ability to lead a godly life?

2. All this changed when you accepted Jesus' sacrifice for your sins and became a member of God's family. Read 2 Peter 1:3–4. At times, you might be tempted to think that you don't have *access* to God's power, especially if you are feeling ineffective in reaching your goals or sense you lack the strength to overcome struggles in your life. But what does this passage say about the type of power you can now access?

3. Read 2 Peter 1:5–9. You have a part to play in embracing the power that God has given you and putting it to use in your life. What are some of the ways that God expects you to grow as a result of possessing His divine power? What are the benefits for those who grow in these qualities? What are the consequences for those who do not?

4. God expects you to grow in His strength. In Luke 2:52, we find even Jesus "grew in wisdom and stature, and in favor with God and man." If Jesus needed to grow and mature, you have to do so as well! You don't have to describe your physical height, but in what ways are you growing in wisdom and favor with God and those around you?

5. Luke notes that Jesus grew in favor with God *and* with man. What does Paul say in Galatians 1:10 and 1 Thessalonians 2:4 about not seeking the approval of people? Given this, what do you think it means to grow in favor with people, like Jesus did?

" *God said,* "Let us make mankind in our image, in our likeness, so that they may rule over the fish in the sea and the birds in the sky, over the livestock and all the wild animals, and over all the creatures that move along the ground."

> So God created mankind in his own image,
>   in the image of God he created them;
>   male and female he created them.

God blessed them and said to them, "Be fruitful and increase in number; fill the earth and subdue it. Rule over the fish in the sea and the birds in the sky and over every living creature that moves on the ground."

— GENESIS 1:26–28

6. Read the passage from Genesis 1:26–28 on the opposite page. Notice from these verses that God did not create humans in a haphazard manner. Rather, you were created by God with purpose and intention. What does it mean to you that you were created in God's own image? How easy or difficult is it for you to see yourself in that way?

7. Given that God does not have a physical form, the only image that humans could possibly bear that resemble their Creator is an inner image—their spirit. How does this shed light on what it means to be created in God's image? If someone were to look at your heart, would they see traits that resemble God? Why or why not?

8. There is another important takeaway from Genesis 1:26–28. What blessing did God give to the first man and woman? What does this blessing say about His original intention for humans as it related to exerting His authority over this world?

The serpent was more crafty than any of the wild animals the LORD God had made. He said to the woman, "Did God really say, 'You must not eat from any tree in the garden'?"

The woman said to the serpent, "We may eat fruit from the trees in the garden, but God did say, 'You must not eat fruit from the tree that is in the middle of the garden, and you must not touch it, or you will die.'"

"You will not certainly die," the serpent said to the woman. "For God knows that when you eat from it your eyes will be opened, and you will be like God, knowing good and evil."

When the woman saw that the fruit of the tree was good for food and pleasing to the eye, and also desirable for gaining wisdom, she took some and ate it. She also gave some to her husband, who was with her, and he ate it.

— GENESIS 3:1–6

9. Clearly, something went wrong. There is a stark contrast between what we were created *for* and what our lives look like today. Read the passage from Genesis 3:1–6 on the opposite page. How did the serpent convince Adam and Eve to lay down their power? What are some of the ways that the enemy tries to steal our power today?

10. Adam and Eve were deceived by the serpent. His words caused them to question God's character, which led to them disobeying the Lord, which resulted in them giving up their authority over the enemy. Take an honest look at your life. Are you allowing the enemy to rob you of the power that you actually have the authority to control?

APPLY WHAT YOU LEARNED

Ultimately, when you get down to it, you are not in a power struggle. If you are a follower of Jesus, you possess God's power. Paul wrote, "The Spirit of him who raised Jesus from the dead is living in you" (Romans 8:11). He also stated, "Your bodies are temples of the Holy Spirit, who is in you, whom you have received from God" (1 Corinthians 6:19).

God's Spirit, and His power, reside within you. So, if you are not experiencing this power, there is an important question you need to ask: *What would it take for me to be honest with God about everything in my life so that He can reach in, restore me to wholeness, and make me aware of the power that is within me?* The world wants to tell you that you are incapable of change—that you have no power to free yourself from unhealthy patterns of behavior. But this is simply not true. You have to stop listening to the enemy's lies and start believing the truths of the power you possess as revealed in God's Word.

In the following questions and exercises, be brutally honest with God. Tell Him everything. He not only can take it but also knows everything already and has been waiting for you to be real with Him. Just like a loving parent, He is just waiting for you, as His child, to come forward with the truth. He is there and is ready to have this conversation.

1. Imagine living in the world of Adam and Eve before the fall, where there was no such thing as "I can't" or "I don't know how to do that." How would your life be different if you had that same kind of confidence in your life? Who would you be if you leaned into that power? Explain your response.

2. Paul wrote, "I can do all this through him who gives me strength" (Philippians 4:13). What makes it difficult for you to believe this? How would changing your mentality from "I can't" to "I can" produce a shift in your perspective?

3. You have to walk *with* power (Jesus) before you can walk *in* power. Consider the example of Peter. When he first dropped his fishing nets to follow Christ (see Luke 5:11), he didn't have the power that he would one day have to preach to a crowd in Jerusalem (see Acts

2:14). How do you think engaging in fellowship with Jesus on a daily basis impacted his power for God's kingdom? What would need to change in your life for you to more regularly connect with Jesus, your power source, each and every day?

4. God's power is not just reserved for moving forward in your life. His power is also available to help you go back and heal what you've tried to leave behind. When you look at your life, what is something from your past that might be holding you down and robbing you of power? How can you bring that past situation to God today?

5. Sometimes, God will bring you into a new season that will require you to embrace a new set of situational values. We see this in the story of Joshua. When God raised up Joshua as a leader, He let him know that his success would depend not on serving—as he had presumably done under Moses—but on being strong (see Joshua 1:6–7). How willing are you to make this kind of change when God brings you into a new season? What do you think you could accomplish if you better accepted this repositioning in your life?

PRAY TO CLOSE

If you are in a group, take time to pray with and for one another. It is vitally important and will bring a sense of connection to the group that only God can provide. Consider the following prayer if you don't quite have the words to wrap around this week of study:

> *Jesus, thank You for giving me the space to come to You in full honesty and trust. I know You have a plan for me to reclaim what I have forfeited or has been taken away from me. You can do all things, and I give my life back to You to be used for Your good intentions. Be ever near me as I walk this road with You. As I start this journey, go before me and behind me to seal what You are transforming in my heart and mind. Thank You, Jesus. Amen.*

LOOKING AHEAD

In session 2, we will look at how our core values can be upheld or torn down by the systems we have in place in our lives. We will get practical about how we can replace old beliefs with new ones that will help lead us into an integrated and authentic life.

Power to Get Unstuck

Read chapters 4–6 in *Power Moves* by Sarah Jakes Roberts.

Big Idea: You do not have to stay stuck where you are. God has given you the ability to take on new beliefs that will replace the old ones holding you back. When put into action, these values can transform your life and the lives of others.

SCAN ME

Scan to hear a word on this session from Sarah.

"Until you decide that you do not deserve the debilitating results that your system constantly produces, you cannot break out of your system. And you can't break out of your system if you don't acknowledge where you keep getting stuck. . . . Every time you make a choice opposite of what your negative systems dictate, you are serving notice to them that they no longer have power. If you want to know whether your system is healthy, you've got to look at the outcome you consistently produce. Even if the outcome is not what you desire, it can help you to better understand what system may be at play.

— SARAH JAKES ROBERTS[5]

Perhaps you think of yourself as a "systems" person. Even if you are not in the computer or technology field, you like having a set process in place. Your systems take the guesswork out of a task and reassure you that all will turn out well in the end.

The world runs on all kinds of systems. There are systems for banking that allow you to manage your money. There are entertainment systems that enable you to listen to music and watch the movies you enjoy. You likely have some form of "health and wellness" system in place that helps you get enough sleep and maintain a healthy lifestyle. But you also have internal systems that help you determine how you act in a given situation.

Sometimes, these internal systems can actually work against you when you are trying to change an unhealthy habit or pursue a goal. For instance, maybe when you were growing up, you learned that it was best to stay out of the way or just be quiet. So now, you find it hard to speak up for yourself, even though that is something you want to do. Or maybe, growing up, you learned it was necessary to speak into every family conversation. So now, you find it hard to listen to the opinions of others, even though that is something you want to do.

How can you get yourself *unstuck* from this problem? The answer is by changing the systems in your brain that are not allowing you to pursue the values in your heart. This will require you to honestly examine any system that you have created—perhaps as a means of survival growing up—that has now become a "virus" keeping you from health.

Think about what happens when a virus infects a computer. Once it has infiltrated a system, it will infect programs, modify or disable core functions, and copy or delete important data. A virus will slow down the computer's functionality and yield undesirable results other than what the user intended. Viruses will eventually render the computer useless.

In a similar way, "viruses" will keep you from living as the person God designed you to be. They will compel you to live up to the standards of others. They will convince you that you can't access the power you need to change. They will give you a false sense of security and keep you stuck in your comfort zones. These viruses can be difficult to recognize. After all, when you get used to feeling down all the time, you don't recognize it as abnormal anymore. You just think it's the way it is. You become comfortable there.

In this session, you will explore how God's Word has made a way for you to identify these viruses. You will look for any comfort zones you have created that are offering you a false sense of security. And you will look at what God says about how you can cultivate a fully integrated life where your beliefs, words, and actions all align with His values.

OPENING PRAYER

Lord, be specific and clear with me as I come honestly before You. Give my spirit the humility to hear what You have to say and accept what You reveal. I am ready to examine the areas of my life that need to change. Show me where to start and encourage me with Your Word. Amen.

BEGINNING QUESTION

To get things started, discuss one of these questions as a group:

- If you could pick a favorite tangible system that you use every day, what would it be? (Note: not everyone can pick a coffee maker!)

— *or* —

- What does it mean for a person to be "stuck" in life?

CONSIDER YOUR LIFE

Merriam-Webster defines the word *stuck* as being "blocked, wedged, or jammed . . . to find oneself baffled . . . to be unable to proceed."[6] For you to reclaim God's power and allow it to move in you, you have to consider whether you are *stuck* in any areas of your life. Answer the following questions to make this assessment and to prepare your heart for this session.

1. How able are you to accomplish daily goals you set for yourself?

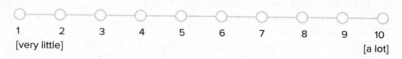

1   2   3   4   5   6   7   8   9   10
[very little]   [a lot]

2. How able are you to move toward larger goals you have in your life?

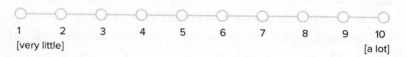

1   2   3   4   5   6   7   8   9   10
[very little]   [a lot]

3. What do you feel is keeping you stuck in these areas?

4. How willing are you to follow God's lead and get unstuck in these areas in your life?

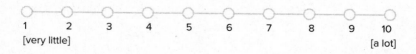

1   2   3   4   5   6   7   8   9   10
[very little]   [a lot]

DISCUSS AS A GROUP

Use the following questions to help you marinate on the main themes from chapters 4–6 of *Power Moves*, engage in discussion, and apply the concepts to your life.

1. Read Romans 6:1–11. What does Paul say in this passage about taking God's grace for granted and remaining stuck in your sin? What happens to your character when you use God's grace as an excuse rather than a launching point for change?

2. What are some of your comfort zones in life? What are they offering you that makes you want to remain in those zones? (Think about your upbringing, culture, or any other influences that helped you create those spaces of comfort.)

3. Consider some of the internal systems that you have developed. Do you need to evaluate any of those systems to make sure they are leading you where God wants you to go? What systems are keeping you from dying to yourself (see verse 11)?

4. Read Titus 2:11–14. If you want to dismantle a long-held negative belief, you have to replace it with a positive belief that you feel is more compelling. Every time you make a choice opposite to what your negative systems dictate, you are serving notice to them that they no longer have power. What power does Paul say that God gives you to say no to ungodliness? What does God enable you to do?

5. Read Romans 8:28. People like to recite the first part of this verse—that "in all things God works for the good" of them. But what are the two qualifications for this promise to be true? How does that change your perspective of what Paul is saying here?

And a woman was there

who had been subject to bleeding for twelve years, but no one could heal her. She came up behind [Jesus] and touched the edge of his cloak, and immediately her bleeding stopped.

"Who touched me?" Jesus asked.

When they all denied it, Peter said, "Master, the people are crowding and pressing against you."

But Jesus said, "Someone touched me; I know that power has gone out from me."

Then the woman, seeing that she could not go unnoticed, came trembling and fell at his feet. In the presence of all the people, she told why she had touched him and how she had been instantly healed. Then he said to her, "Daughter, your faith has healed you. Go in peace."

LUKE 8:43–48

6. Read the passage from Luke 8:43–48 on the opposite page. What was the woman's system of operation? How do you imagine that she lived every day? What compelling belief did she have deep inside that ultimately prompted her to move toward action?

7. Read the parallel account of this story found in Matthew 9:20–22. This woman took a great risk in approaching Jesus and touching His cloak. Under Jewish law, her bleeding meant that she was considered to be ceremonially unclean. But what did she believe would happen if she could just touch Jesus' cloak? Do you have this same kind of faith in God's character when you are desperate for a touch from Him? Explain your response.

8. What did Jesus say went out of Him when the woman touched the edge of His cloak (see Luke 8:46)? What did Jesus say brought healing to the woman (see verse 48)?

❝ [Esther] instructed [the king's eunuch] to say to Mordecai, "All the king's officials and the people of the royal provinces know that for any man or woman who approaches the king in the inner court without being summoned the king has but one law: that they be put to death unless the king extends the gold scepter to them and spares their lives. But thirty days have passed since I was called to go to the king."

When Esther's words were reported to Mordecai, he sent back this answer: "Do not think that because you are in the king's house you alone of all the Jews will escape. For if you remain silent at this time, relief and deliverance for the Jews will arise from another place, but you and your father's family will perish. And who knows but that you have come to your royal position for such a time as this?"

Then Esther sent this reply to Mordecai: "Go, gather together all the Jews who are in Susa, and fast for me. Do not eat or drink for three days, night or day. I and my attendants will fast as you do. When this is done, I will go to the king, even though it is against the law. And if I perish, I perish."

ESTHER 4:10–16

9. Read the passage from Esther 4:10–16 on the opposite page. This scene represents the pinnacle of Esther's story, where she decided to approach the king of Persia and plead for him to spare the Jews from annihilation. What system had she found comfort in? What did she know to be the consequences if she moved outside of that system?

10. What did Mordecai say to Esther that caused her to take on a more compelling belief than the one she had? What values did she lean on when facing this extremely delicate and difficult situation? What core values would you say define your life?

APPLY WHAT YOU LEARNED

Paul wrote, "Do not conform to the pattern of this world, but be transformed by the renewing of your mind" (Romans 12:2). Every day, you are bombarded with messages from the media, from politicians, from special interest groups, and from society as a whole that insinuates you have to conform to their way of thinking and their set of beliefs. Not all of those messages are bad. Many call you to be a responsible and informed citizen—which is a good thing. But you should never allow those messages to lead you into *conforming* with the world.

James wrote, "Friendship with the world means enmity against God" (James 4:4). You are not called to do things the world's way. But you can't be transformed and follow God's way if you don't take the time to really know the Author of your story. God has designed you in His image, as you explored in the last session, and you have to keep your mind fixed on Him to not allow yourself to be conformed to the world. As Paul stated, "'Who has known the mind of the Lord so as to instruct him?' But we have the mind of Christ" (1 Corinthians 2:16).

You have the mind of Christ! His power *can* transform you. You no longer have to be trapped in the world's systems that hold you in bondage. Consider this truth as you work through the following questions and apply what you have learned in this session.

1. What are some of the systems of the world that you have seen that run contrary to God's Word? Which of these systems might have gained a foothold in your life?

2. One definition of the word *pattern* is "traits, acts, tendencies, or other observable characteristics of a person, group, or institution."[7] What does this definition say about why it is often so hard to break free and get unstuck from a pattern?

3. What is one practical thing you can do this week to break free from a pattern of the world and begin the process of allowing God to renew your mind?

4. Paul stated that when you have a renewed mind, "you will be able to test and approve what God's will is—his good, pleasing and perfect will" (Romans 12:2). How do you think this process works? How does a renewed mind lead to you knowing God's will?

5. Tomorrow is not guaranteed. "You are a mist that appears for a little while and then vanishes" (James 4:14). So it is important to consider how you are living *today*. What are some of God's values that you would like to be a greater part of your character?

PRAY TO CLOSE

Jesus, thank You for tearing down systems that keep me from You. Thank You for exposing the systems in me that I believed for so long . . . only to find they were hindering my intimacy with You. There is no striving with You, Lord, but out of my love for You, I want to live my life in a way that I am worthy of the calling You have given me. Help me to embrace the power You have placed into my life as I seek Your will to be done on earth as it is in heaven. Amen.

LOOKING AHEAD

So far, we have learned how God's power moves *in* us. Starting in session 3, we are going to focus on how God's power moves *through* us. We will confront how God actually wants to use us and how He has empowered us to accomplish great things for Him.

Power to Be Used by God

Read chapters 7–9 in *Power Moves* by Sarah Jakes Roberts.

Big Idea: You've done some hard inner work. Now it's time to see where God wants to put you to work. Yes, He desires you to rise to the occasion, meet needs in other people's lives, and fill the voids in the way that only you can. He gives you power to accomplish His purposes.

SCAN ME

Scan to hear a word on this session from Sarah.

God did not call you to success without scars. God has called you to the sacred journey of trusting Him through failure and disappointment. Maybe you should stop asking yourself if you can change and still be great and instead begin asking yourself if you can stay the same and still experience God's new mercy. The old voices of fear and shame that once haunted and taunted you will surrender to the knowledge you are being made whole. . . . You will be informing your doubt, worry, shame, and fear that their power has moved, and you're determined to move with it.

— SARAH JAKES ROBERTS [8]

S cars mean something. They usually indicate that something significant has happened in a person's life. A tumble down the stairs. A bite from an animal. A cut on the skin.

Every scar tells a story. Yet not all scars exist because of something negative. Some represent new life coming into the world, like the gift of sharing an organ with another person. Some represent a tragic event that was avoided, like the scars received by someone who saved another person's life.

Jesus had scars. The scars that He received on the cross were for the purpose of saving lives. Paul wrote, "For the wages of sin is death, but the gift of God is eternal life in Christ Jesus our Lord" (Romans 6:23). Every person on earth was destined for the tragic event of spiritual separation from God. But Jesus' scars brought the hope of *eternal* life for all who receive His offer.

In the Gospels, we see that Jesus did not shy away from showing His scars. "Look at my hands and my feet," He said to the disciples after the resurrection. "It is I myself! Touch me and see; a ghost does not have flesh and bones, as you see I have" (Luke 24:39). The first thing that Jesus did when He saw His disciples was show them His scars! He would later also say to Thomas—the disciple who doubted He was alive—"Put your finger here; see my hands. Reach out your hand and put it into my side. Stop doubting and believe" (John 20:27).

Jesus received His scars "by becoming obedient to death" (Philippians 2:8). So it would be foolish for us to think we can make it through this life without at least some scrapes and bruises along the way. But the interesting thing about scars is that they are not a permanent fixture in the body. After the scar heals, the body goes through a "remodeling" process. The body rebuilds the scar so it becomes stronger and more like the surrounding tissue.

God will use the scars we receive in our obedience to Him to make us stronger. Slowly, over time, He will remodel us and strengthen us. He will use our scars to reveal to others that we understand what they are going through—for we were once there ourselves. He will use the situations we have gone through to prepare us for His service and fill the voids in other people's lives. His power will change not only our own lives but also the lives around us. Power is never meant to stay locked up in us. It is to be used in the manner that God deems best.

We discussed previously how God gave Adam and Eve the command to "fill the earth" (Genesis 1:28). This implies there was something empty that needed to be filled. We see a lot of emptiness in our world today. Souls that are empty. Bustling cities that are empty. Even full churches with leaders who are empty. The command remains for us to "fill the earth." God doesn't ask us to live as bystanders or ignore what we could be changing. Rather, He prepares us—sometimes through our scars—to be a powerful force for Him in this world.

OPENING PRAYER

Father, help me to see how You have given me power that is to be used for Your glory. Nothing makes You happier than people coming to know You. Help me to have open hands and an open mind to how You may be asking me to make the most of my scars. Prepare me to point others to the fullness found only in You so that I can be the solution that You are calling me to be. Amen.

BEGINNING QUESTION

To get things started, discuss one of these questions as a group:

- What is the story behind a physical scar that you have?

— *or* —

- What does it mean to live as a bystander in this world?

CONSIDER YOUR LIFE

Oswald Chambers wrote, "The things we try to avoid and fight against—tribulation, suffering, and persecution—are the very things that produce abundant joy in us."[9] In this session, you will explore how God will use your scars to accomplish His plans. Use the following questions to assess the state of your heart before you go deeper into the subject matter.

1. What "scars" are you carrying? List a few that come to mind.

2. How open are you to sharing the scars you've received with others?

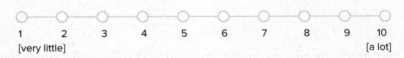

1   2   3   4   5   6   7   8   9   10
[very little]   [a lot]

3. What is your primary reluctance, if any, to sharing these scars?

4. How likely are you to be obedient to God if it means that you will go through pain?

1   2   3   4   5   6   7   8   9   10
[very little]   [a lot]

DISCUSS AS A GROUP

Use the following questions to help you marinate on the main themes from chapters 7–9 of *Power Moves*, engage in discussion, and apply the concepts to your life.

1. Read Isaiah 53:5. What assurance do you have in the wounds that Jesus suffered on your behalf? Can you imagine your scars bringing healing to others?

2. In the list of the scars you made, are any still causing you shame, guilt, or regret? If so, you might be tempted to hide these scars and not let anyone truly know or see you. But you have freedom in Christ, who gives you life through His scars. What are some positive ways that the scars you have could become a source of strength?

3. Turn to 2 Corinthians 11:24–28. What are some of the scars that Paul endured in his mission to spread the gospel? How do you think that Paul found the strength to continue on in his mission in spite of all the trials that he faced?

4. Read John 6:35–38. What did Jesus understand about His mission that others were unwilling to see? What do you think made Jesus so confident in His mission? How can you likewise develop confidence in the mission that God has called you to perform?

5. Now look at Genesis 2:8–9, 15–17. What mission did God give to Adam and Eve? What was required on their part to participate in this mission and see it succeed?

" Dear friends, do not believe every spirit, but test the spirits to see whether they are from God, because many false prophets have gone out into the world. This is how you can recognize the Spirit of God: Every spirit that acknowledges that Jesus Christ has come in the flesh is from God, but every spirit that does not acknowledge Jesus is not from God. This is the spirit of the antichrist, which you have heard is coming and even now is already in the world.

You, dear children, are from God and have overcome them, because the one who is in you is greater than the one who is in the world.

1 JOHN 4:1–4

6. Read the passage from 1 John 4:1–4 on the opposite page. None of us are strangers to feelings of inadequacy when it comes to our personal lives. What do these verses promise you when you face people and situations that are bigger than you?

7. John states that we are to "test the spirits" (verse 1). In his day, followers of Jesus were being led astray by teachers who were proclaiming a gospel that was different than the one that he and the apostles were proclaiming. This was a false spirit. How does John say that we can know the difference between a true and a false spirit?

8. John states that "the spirit of the antichrist" is already at work in the world to deceive true followers of Christ (verse 3). But what power do we have over this spirit?

"If you keep your feet
from breaking the Sabbath
and from doing as you please on my
holy day,
if you call the Sabbath a delight
and the LORD's holy day honorable,
and if you honor it by not going your
own way
and not doing as you please or speaking
idle words,
then you will find your joy in the LORD,
and I will cause you to ride in triumph
on the heights of the land
and to feast on the inheritance of your
father Jacob."
For the mouth of the LORD has spoken.

ISAIAH 58:13–14

9. Read the passage from Isaiah 58:13–14 on the opposite page. God had instructed the Israelites to keep one day of the week—the Sabbath—holy by not doing any work on that day (see Exodus 20:8–11). Why do you think God commanded the Sabbath to be observed? What is the benefit to you in keeping a Sabbath day of rest?

10. Sometimes, being powerful is admitting you're tired, overwhelmed, angry, confused, or stuck. In a world that applauds relentless productivity, sometimes the most powerful thing you can do is rest. Is taking a Sabbath a regular part of your life, or do you find it difficult to rest? How could nonstop activity be working against you?

APPLY WHAT YOU LEARNED

In this session, you explored how there will be times when God will call you to radical obedience. He will ask you to step away from your comfort zones so that you can step up and fill voids in other people's lives that only you can fill. Elisha was called to this kind of obedience.

When we first encounter Elisha, he was leading an average and comfortable life. "He was plowing with twelve yoke of oxen, and he himself was driving the twelfth pair" (1 Kings 19:19). But then the prophet Elijah appeared and threw his cloak over him, effectively naming him his successor. At this point, Elisha had a decision to make: stay where it was comfortable or take a risk and be used by God. Elisha made his choice. He said goodbye to his family, burned his plowing equipment, slaughtered his oxen, and fed the neighborhood on his way out. He would go on to fill the void left by Elijah when the prophet was taken to heaven.

Elisha would be used powerfully by God in this role. He directed kings during a tumultuous time in Israel's history and warned the people of the consequences of their idolatry. He performed many miracles through God's power, including healing the waters of Jericho (see 2 Kings 2:19–21), multiplying a widow's oil (see 4:1–7), and removing poison from a pot of stew (see 4:38–41). All because Elisha was willing to leave his comfortable life behind. Consider the example of Elisha's life as you work through the following questions.

1. When you read of people in the Bible like Elijah and Elisha, it can be tempting to think they were "special" in some way that allowed God to use them as He did. But the truth is, they were average people just like you (see James 5:17). So what made the difference in their ability to be used so powerfully by God? What does that say to you?

2. Be completely honest with yourself as you answer this next question. Are you committed to the same kind of obedience to God that you find in Elisha's story? If not, what small step can you take today that will lead toward that level of obedience?

3. Can you say the sphere of your world looks any different because of the way you interact with it? Do you complain, divide, tear others down, and feel sorry for yourself—or do you love, give your time and resources, show compassion, and rejoice in others? What is one thing you can stop this week and one thing you can start this week?

4. What, if anything, is holding you back from being obedient to what God has called you to do and being the solution to a problem you see that bothers you?

5. We don't know much about Elisha before he met Elijah, but he clearly had a trust in God that made him stand out from others. After all, the Lord handpicked him to be Elijah's successor (see 1 Kings 19:16). Elisha's trust in God enabled him to step into a world with which he was unfamiliar and solve problems. How would you rate your trust in God? When you come to Him for guidance, do you linger and wait to hear His voice, or do you try to manipulate your own desired outcome? Explain your response.

PRAY TO CLOSE

Father, show me where You want me to step up, fill voids, and lead in the world around me. Help me to have the same willing spirit as Elisha, who was ready to leave everything of comfort behind to follow You. Use the scars I have received to help me relate to those who are hurting and for Your glory. Although I know more scars are in my future, I trust You, Lord, to lead me. Fill me afresh with Your truth and provide me with Your rest. Amen.

LOOKING AHEAD

In session 4, we will examine how God has given us power to engage in spiritual warfare against our enemy. We will see how God connects us with our fellow brothers and sisters in Christ to build us up and enable us to counter the enemy's attacks.

Power to Engage in Battle

Read chapters 10–12 in *Power Moves* by Sarah Jakes Roberts.

Big Idea: You are going to face hard things in life, and your response to those challenges will say a lot about your relationship with Christ and your trust in Him. Regardless of the circumstance, you were never meant to face it on your own. Your enemy can be defeated through your connection with Christ and with help from your fellow believers.

SCAN ME

Scan to hear a word on this session from Sarah.

The enemy works hard to keep you from allowing the life of Jesus to transform the way you view your life. You'll notice that the moment you begin to walk in truth and wisdom, it feels like all kinds of distractions are in your way. You're not going crazy; the force is real. It is trying to keep you from true relationship with Jesus and from having a heart posture that receives a perfect love that casts out fear. In the moments when you begin to feel the strain from this real opposition, you have an opportunity to enact a force that has nothing to do with physical practices and everything to do with spiritual awareness.

— SARAH JAKES ROBERTS[10]

Have you ever been pulled into an argument by default? You didn't even know how you got there. You were minding your own business when, seemingly out of nowhere, someone approached you with a complaint, and soon you found yourself engaged in a heated debate. Or maybe the problem is that you *allowed* yourself to get pulled into an argument. You saw it coming and knew you should avoid it . . . but you didn't.

If either of these scenarios has happened to you, then know that you are in good company. In the Bible, we read how Jesus—immediately after His baptism and start of His public ministry—"was led by the Spirit into the wilderness" (Matthew 4:1). Jesus went there to fast and pray for forty days, and as you might imagine after that length of time, He was quite hungry. It was then, seemingly out of nowhere, that the devil appeared. Satan believed that Jesus was at His weakest, and so he offered up several temptations in an attempt to derail His mission.

The enemy still does this today. He is out to get us and render us ineffective, and he strikes when he feels we are at our weakest. He comes at us in all sorts of ways—but none of these ways are really new. Jesus' example in the wilderness helps us understand how to counter his attacks. We might feel we are weak, but we actually have the power of God available to us at all times. Jesus countered every argument the enemy brought against Him with the truth that is found in God's Word. He had authority over the enemy.

The same in true of us today. We know the enemy's tactics. We understand we have the authority over him. We combat his schemes with the truth of God's Word. We profess that we are children of God who have His power. We sing praises to the Lord and call on Him for help. Prayer and worship are our weapons in a supernatural fight against the darkness.

We also refuse to allow the enemy to fill our heads with his lies. This was the mistake that Eve made. She allowed herself to get pulled into an argument with the devil that she never should have been in. Soon, she was reasoning with what she was meant to have dominion over. God had commanded her to rule and subdue the earth with Adam, yet the serpent slithered his way into her ear. She didn't rely on the truth of God's spoken word to her. Instead, she gave the devil a foothold. The rest is history . . . our history.

So, we know how the enemy works. But it can still be hard to spot his attacks in our lives. We don't always recognize when we're living off the mark or starting to question our God-given authority. This is why we need other faithful followers of Christ in our lives. When we surround ourselves with people we trust and with whom our values align, we take them seriously when they speak into our lives. These relationships help us to spot and counter the enemy's attacks. This is what we will study in this session.

OPENING PRAYER

Father, thank You for the power that is released when I speak out of Your Word. It causes the darkness to flee, the peace to roll in, and reassures me that there is no God but You. Help me to not reason with what You gave me authority over but to counter the enemy's attacks with Your truth. I come with confidence today that You will do what You say You will do. Amen.

BEGINNING QUESTION

To get things started, discuss one of these questions as a group:

- What is a recent argument you had that you got pulled into by default?

— *or* —

- What is a recent argument you had that you now realize you should have avoided?

CONSIDER YOUR LIFE

In this session, you will be taking a look at some of the ways the enemy tries to attack your God-given power. You will consider any ways that you are falling to his attacks. You will also study some strategies in God's power for battling back against the enemy. Before you begin, take the following assessment to consider where you are currently in the fight.

1. How would you describe the degree to which you are being attacked by the enemy?

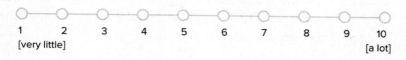

1   2   3   4   5   6   7   8   9   10
[very little]   [a lot]

2. How would you describe the degree to which the enemy has been successful in these attacks?

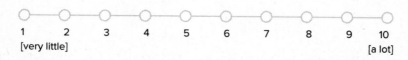

1   2   3   4   5   6   7   8   9   10
[very little]   [a lot]

3. What are some of the areas where you feel weak in your defense?

4. How willing are you to share your struggles with other people in your life and allow them to not only keep you accountable but also help you stand against the enemy's attacks?

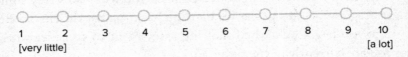

1   2   3   4   5   6   7   8   9   10
[very little]   [a lot]

DISCUSS AS A GROUP

Use the following questions to help you marinate on the main themes from chapters 10–12 of *Power Moves*, engage in discussion, and apply the concepts to your life.

1. Read 1 Peter 5:8 and 2 Corinthians 11:14. Many people today doubt that Satan is real, but the Bible is clear he not only *exists* but also is *active*. What do these verses say about how Satan is at work today?

2. Satan's goal is to keep you as a follower of Christ from pursuing your God-given mission. He is the ultimate "detractor" in that he will use every means available to render you incapable of clinging to the faith, power, and focus that is required for your mission. Read Genesis 3:1–5. What question did the serpent ask Eve? How do you see him using this question to detract Eve from the mission that God had given to her in the garden?

3. Turn to 1 Corinthians 10:12. In the story in Genesis, Eve never volunteered to show off her power. She wasn't seeking an encounter with Satan in an attempt to prove her power to him. What does this say about how God wants you to use your power? What does Paul say is the danger when it comes to thinking you are strong?

4. Now look up Matthew 4:1–11 and read the entire story of Jesus' temptation in the wilderness. Just as with Eve, the enemy tried to distract Jesus from His mission by getting Him to focus on some deficiency. He tried to convince Jesus that He lacked something that God was not providing. How did Jesus respond to these attacks?

5. When you consider this strategy of the enemy, what might be some perceived areas of lack in your life where Satan could launch an attack? In your relationships? Your family? Your finances? Your resources? How can you counter these attacks with God's truth?

Live in harmony with one another. Do not be proud, but be willing to associate with people of low position. Do not be conceited.

ROMANS 12:16

"The greatest among you will be your servant. For those who exalt themselves will be humbled, and those who humble themselves will be exalted."

MATTHEW 23:11–12

"Whoever wants to become great among you must be your servant, and whoever wants to be first must be slave of all."

MARK 10:43–44

"Give, and it will be given to you. A good measure, pressed down, shaken together and running over, will be poured into your lap. For with the measure you use, it will be measured to you."

LUKE 6:38

"Whoever serves me must follow me; and where I am, my servant also will be. My Father will honor the one who serves me."

JOHN 12:26

6. Read through the verses on the opposite page. What recurring theme stands out to you? In your own life, do you feel the need to be applauded and cheered on for your victories? Is there something inside you that needs to be recognized? Explain.

7. What does Paul say in Romans 12:16 about the way in which followers of Jesus are to treat others? Do you find it hard to truly live in harmony with others? Explain.

8. How did Jesus consistently answer when asked about which posture of the heart pleases God the most? What did Jesus say that greatness means in the kingdom of God?

"Let us hold unswervingly
to the hope we profess, for he who promised
is faithful. And let us consider how we may
spur one another on toward love and good
deeds, not giving up meeting together,
as some are in the habit of doing, but
encouraging one another—and all the more
as you see the Day approaching. . . .
You need to persevere so that when you
have done the will of God, you will receive
what he has promised.

HEBREWS 10:23–25, 36

9. Read the passage from Hebrews 10 on the opposite page. What are some of the ways that you are spurring on your fellow brothers and sisters in Christ toward love and good deeds? Why is it so important to persevere in this mission?

10. Read Romans 14:13. The influence of others can be powerful. When have you experienced a "stumbling block" because of what someone else did or said? How might you have put a stumbling block in someone else's life because of your decisions?

APPLY WHAT YOU LEARNED

"Pride goes before destruction" (Proverbs 16:18). Pride is dangerous because it keeps us from engaging with others in the way that God intended and reaching out to them for help. Pride hampers our effectiveness in the battle against our enemy. For this reason, we need to have a strategy in place for how to combat pride when we see it rear its ugly head.

One such strategy is found in Acts 16:22–36. Paul and Silas were in Philippi when they were falsely accused, beaten, and thrown into prison. But when they arrived there, they didn't sulk or try to convince others they were innocent. Instead, they prayed and sang hymns of worship to God. The next thing you know, the doors were flying open and the chains were falling off. The jailer saw what was happening and, thinking the prisoners had fled, was about to take his own life. But Paul, laying down his pride, said they were all there. The jailer then fell before them and asked what he must do to be saved.

Paul and Silas fought back against the enemy with prayer and worship. As a result, the jailer and his household came to salvation in Christ Jesus—and Paul and Silas were set free. But it's important to see that this didn't come about as a result of them pressing their authority. It came through humble submission to God and a willingness to allow Him to fight their battles. Consider these truths as you work through the following questions.

1. Have you ever been in a situation where it seemed the *last* logical thing to do was worship God and express your praise to Him? What does the story of Paul and Silas reveal about how God can move in your life when you choose worship over worry?

2. Implement this praise-and-worship strategy by finding a worship playlist on a streaming service. (See the QR code included in this guide for a link to a Spotify playlist from Sarah.) Have it queued up and ready to go when the need arises. Now write a one-sentence prayer that is short enough to memorize and say back to God when you feel the enemy is coming against you. Include Scripture in your prayer. For example, *Lord, You are my strength and my shield. I trust in You. I give thanks to You in spite of this circumstance* (see Psalm 28:7).

3. Worship also has the benefit of taking the focus off yourself and putting it on God. How can even this act help you to maintain an attitude of humility and avoid pride?

4. One of the Ten Commandments is to not *covet* (see Exodus 20:17). Coveting stems from pride in that it encourages us to compare ourselves to others and conclude that we are lacking in something. Why do you think it is often so hard to rejoice in other people's successes? What could you do this week to show that you are laying down your pride and cheering on another person's win?

5. Jesus said this about your enemy: "He was a murderer from the beginning, not holding to the truth, for there is no truth in him. When he lies, he speaks his native language, for he is a liar and the father of lies" (John 8:44). What lies might the enemy be telling you today about your worth to God? What truth from God's Word can you use to combat these lies (see, for example, Psalm 139:15–16; Matthew 10:31; John 1:12; 1 Peter 2:9)?

PRAY TO CLOSE

Father, place in my mind what You say is true about me. Help me to converge with Your Spirit and allow Your power to be on display through me. I arrest my pride and lay myself down at Your feet to be used for Your will. Let prayer and worship become my default as I navigate life with You. Use me powerfully to bring others to Yourself in the world around me. Amen.

LOOKING AHEAD

As we move on to session 5, we will explore how our connection with God enables us to see what He is doing behind the scenes in our world. We will see that as we allow God to change our way of thinking, nothing is impossible for us as we rely on His power.

SESSION FIVE

Power to See God Move

Read chapters 13–15 in *Power Moves* by Sarah Jakes Roberts.

Big Idea: God will use things within your reach to solve problems in ways that you could never imagine. When you allow your mindset to shift from one in which you continually feel defeated to one in which you see challenging situations as an opportunity for God to do something new, you will get a front seat to see what God is doing.

Scan to hear a word on
this session from Sarah.

When you draw closer to God, it doesn't just initiate a journey of bearing God's image on earth; it also grants you access to God's plans for the earth. . . . When you refuse to believe that you serve a God who would leave you in the dark, you search Scriptures, sermons, worship songs, and meditations until you begin to see light flickering again. The pursuit of God's perspective is not just about reconciling your past and making peace with your present. God's perspective also carries with it innovation for how your gifts and talents align with what God wants to see happen in the earth.

— SARAH JAKES ROBERTS[11]

S cientists tell us that humans see the world according to the way their brains organize its elements—such as shapes, sizes, colors, and spatial relationships.[12] Our brains store information on how objects "should" look, feel, taste, sound, or smell based on past sensory information. It's why we can look up at clouds and see recognizable shapes like horses, rabbits, or the faces of people—a phenomenon that scientists call pareidolia.[13]

The same holds true when it comes to us determining what is possible in our world. We have a preconceived set of beliefs that we use to determine what is rational or not. But what happens when God reveals something that runs counter to our human perceptions? What happens what God asks us to do something that makes no logical sense to us? How much are we willing to risk on God, surrender to Him, and do exactly what He has told us to do?

In the Old Testament, we read a story about a man named Naaman. He was a foreign commander who was stricken with leprosy. When he learned there was a prophet of God in Israel named Elisha who could provide healing to him, Naaman set off to see him. But Elisha only sent messengers to Naaman with instructions to wash seven times in the Jordan River.

Naaman grew angry. Why? The method of healing didn't make sense. After all, there were better rivers in his own land where he could wash than the muddy Jordan. Naaman had his own perceptions about how the healing should occur . . . something a bit more flashy and showy. So he determined to just go back home. Thankfully, he had servants who cared about him and who were willing to open their minds to what God could do. They convinced Naaman to follow Elisha's instructions, and his skin became like that of a young boy (see 2 Kings 5).

Naaman's story reveals that God does not work according to a formula. Just because He is the same "yesterday and today and forever" (Hebrews 13:8) does not mean that we can put Him in a box.

So when He gives us a solution to a problem that runs contrary to what we thought the solution would be, it is an opportunity for us to put our faith in Him. We get to choose if we are going to allow our own perceptions to hold us back or if we are willing to open our eyes to see what God sees. Sometimes, this means heading into battle. Other times, it means accepting the Lord's rest and allowing Him to fight the battle for us (see Exodus 14:14).

Naaman's story also reveals that the Lord will put people into our lives who will encourage us to be open to God's plans. We just need to do the work of setting up proper boundaries in our lives so we can foster those kinds of honest relationships. As we will explore in this session, as we allow God to take us out of our comfort zones, stretch our perceptions of what is possible, and listen to those He has put into our lives, we will see Him move in powerful ways.

OPENING PRAYER

Father, meet me in this moment. As I think back on circumstances beyond my control or problems with no solution, teach me how to seek Your heart and be open to whatever direction You want to take. Your ways are higher and more than I can understand, but I trust You. Help me to see where You are working and what You are asking me to do. Amen.

BEGINNING QUESTION

To get things started, discuss one of these questions as a group:

- When is a time in your life that things were not as they initially seemed?

  — *or* —

- When is a time in your life that God revealed something miraculous to you?

CONSIDER YOUR LIFE

God said to us, "My thoughts are not your thoughts, neither are your ways my ways" (Isaiah 55:8). Yet how often we try to fit God into a box! We prefer it when He acts in ways that make sense to us—and when He acts in ways that don't move us out of our comfort zones. As we begin to explore these topics in this session, take a few moments to evaluate how open you are to seeing God move and how willing you are to follow His movements wherever they lead.

1. How would you describe your ability to hear God's voice?

1	2	3	4	5	6	7	8	9	10
[very little]									[a lot]

2. How willing are you to move outside of your comfort zones?

1	2	3	4	5	6	7	8	9	10
[very little]									[a lot]

3. What is something that God has revealed to you recently that has gone against your expectations?

4. How willing are you to obey God in spite of not understanding where He is leading you?

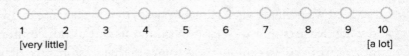

1   2   3   4   5   6   7   8   9   10

[very little]   [a lot]

DISCUSS AS A GROUP

Use the following questions to help you marinate on the main themes from chapters 13–15 of *Power Moves*, engage in discussion, and apply the concepts to your life.

1. Read Proverbs 25:2. This verse provides insight into how God functions. What does it mean that God conceals things from us? God sees the whole picture and we just see a part, so what can you know to be true if He isn't revealing everything to you?

2. Think of a dream or desire that God has placed in your heart that has not yet come to pass. What does this verse encourage you to do? How might God be working in any disappointments in your life to prepare you for the future that He has for you?

3. Look up James 1:5–8. What should you do when you feel that you are in the dark concerning God's plans? Why do you think James adds that when you ask God for wisdom, you should not doubt but believe that He will provide it to you?

4. Read Ephesians 3:14–19. Paul was praying for the believers in the city of Ephesus when he wrote these words. How many times does Paul mention *power* in this passage? What did Paul want the power of God to enable the believers to do?

5. What do you think it means to be "filled to the measure of all the fullness of God" (verse 19)? What are some ways that you seek this kind of "filling" from God?

"Jesus went up on a mountainside and called to him those he wanted, and they came to him. He appointed twelve that they might be with him and that he might send them out to preach and to have authority to drive out demons. . . .

Then Jesus entered a house, and again a crowd gathered, so that he and his disciples were not even able to eat. When his family heard about this, they went to take charge of him, for they said, "He is out of his mind." . . .

Then Jesus' mother and brothers arrived. Standing outside, they sent someone in to call him. A crowd was sitting around him, and they told him, "Your mother and brothers are outside looking for you."

"Who are my mother and my brothers?" he asked.

Then he looked at those seated in a circle around him and said, "Here are my mother and my brothers! Whoever does God's will is my brother and sister and mother."

MARK 3:13–15, 20–21, 31–35

6. Read the passage from Mark 3 on the opposite page. These verses describe some of the early events that occurred when Jesus stepped into the fullness of His ministry. What connection did Jesus make with His disciples? What did He empower them to do?

7. Jesus' act of stepping into His ministry created connection with His disciples but disconnection with His family. How did they react when they heard what Jesus was doing? What did Jesus understand had changed when He looked at those gathered around Him and said, "Here are my mother and my brothers" (verse 34)?

8. When Jesus went from possessing power to releasing power, it changed who He connected with in His social circle. When have you witnessed the same thing happen in your life? Why are such disruptions and disconnections often a sign of development?

"For this reason I remind you
to fan into flame the gift of God, which
is in you through the laying on of my hands.
For the Spirit God gave us does not make
us timid, but gives us power, love and
self-discipline. So do not be ashamed of the
testimony about our Lord or of me his
prisoner. Rather, join with me in suffering for
the gospel, by the power of God.

2 TIMOTHY 1:6–8

9. Read the passage from 2 Timothy 1:6–8 on the opposite page. Stepping into the fullness of God's power will require courage on your part. What does Paul say the Holy Spirit will provide when you are walking in step with Him and going with the flow of His current?

10. Paul encourages Timothy to join with him in "suffering for the gospel" (verse 8). God can't multiply what you are not willing to sacrifice. When have you seen God move because of something you were willing to sacrifice or leave behind? What new seasons has God brought you into because of your willingness to move with Him?

APPLY WHAT YOU LEARNED

What are some of the boxes that people try to put you into? Is it a box labeled *shy*? *Insecure*? *Controlling*? *Weak*? *Complacent*? The truth is that you are a combination of experiences, natural tendencies, personality, and—most of all—divine creation. You are impossible to define because God never meant for you to be painted into a corner. You were purposely designed. So, just as God can't be put in a box, you shouldn't let others put you into a box.

It is important to believe that God *can* use you for His plans and to make yourself available to Him. In John 6:1–14, we read the story of Jesus feeding the five thousand. The disciples had zero faith that they would be able to find enough food to feed the crowds. All they had to work with was a donation of a boy's lunch of five barley loaves and two small fish. Andrew summed up the collective skepticism: "How far will they go among so many?" (verse 9).

Jesus stretched the disciples' minds that day. He took the lunch the boy had made available for His use and multiplied it to the extent that there were leftovers after all the people were fed. He does the same today with what we make available to Him. He takes our gifts and talents and stretches our minds as to what He can accomplish with them. All it takes is a willing spirit. Consider these ideas as you work through the following questions.

1. God promised, "You will seek me and find me when you seek me with all your heart" (Jeremiah 29:13). When you refuse to believe that you serve a God who leaves you in the dark, it motivates you to seek Him. Spend a few moments doing this right now. Turn everything off, get in a quiet place, and listen for what God brings to the surface. After a few minutes have passed, write down what you sensed that God was revealing to you.

2. David made this request of God: "Do not hide your face from me . . . . Do not reject me or forsake me, God my Savior" (Psalm 27:9). David understood God to be his helper and Savior. Where do you need God to show up in your life right now? How can you more actively engage with God in your circumstances?

3. Think back to the story of the boy giving up his lunch for Jesus' use in feeding the five thousand. What is something that you are willing to open up and make available to God for His use—however small it might seem to you? What do you think God could do if you made yourself available to Him in that way?

4. Jesus said to His disciples, "Freely you have received; freely give" (Matthew 10:8). What particular gifts do you believe you have received from God that could be put to use in helping others? How freely do you share those gifts with others? Explain.

5. The disciples had seen Jesus perform many miracles in the past, yet they still doubted that God would provide a way for the problem in the present. How does remembering God's past acts of faithfulness bolster your trust in Him for today? What would it take for God to open your eyes, like He did for the disciples, to see what He can do?

PRAY TO CLOSE

Father, thank You for showing me the truth of Your heart. I hold fast to the fact that You created me in a certain way for greater purposes than I can fathom. Help me to seek You with all my heart. Help me to use the gifts that You have freely given me to help others. Help me to see the world with eyes of faith and walk in the freedom that Jesus has purchased for me. Amen.

LOOKING AHEAD

In this study, we have discussed how God's power moves *in* us and *through* us. Now, in the final session, we will examine how God's power should flow *out* from us to impact the lives of others. God intends for His power to be shared!

SESSION · SIX

Power to Change Lives

Read chapters 16–18 in *Power Moves* by Sarah Jakes Roberts.

Big Idea: God doesn't intend for you to receive His power and then just keep it to yourself. Rather, He wants His power to flow through you so that it can impact the lives of others. But for this to happen, people need to see something authentic in your life they can believe in.

Scan to hear a word on this session from Sarah.

"Go from being a seeker of power to a vessel of power. There comes a moment when you're not just going with the flow anymore. You've actually become the flow. When someone encounters you, they're having a radical encounter with your authenticity and vulnerability. You should expect that you're carrying light with you wherever you go. You should not be surprised when people begin to say that they feel better, calmer, more hopeful once they've been in your presence. That is the byproduct and overflow of what happens when we learn to seek the face of God and to project God's face in all that we see and do. Unleashing your light gives other people permission to do the same.

— SARAH JAKES ROBERTS[14]

In order for a new home to be fully operational and ready to be put on the market, the builders first have to connect it to the local electrical grid. When that step is completed—and only then—all the electrical plugs and switches that the builders have installed will function. But one other step is needed. For the home to not get overloaded with all the power flowing in from the grid, the builders have to install circuit breakers to protect it.

God has made His power available to you. He is like the electrical grid that enables everything in your life to function. Yet God doesn't intend for you to just receive His power and keep it to yourself. This would be like having a lamp in your home that you never plug in to the outlet. No, God wants you to "plug in" to His power so that you can be a light for others. Over time as you do this, you will move from being *in* the flow of power to *becoming* the flow.

However, just as in a home, there will be problems if you don't have some kind of "circuit breaker" in place. A huge part of being able to walk in God's power is *humility*. Those who are effectively used by God are aware of the incredible power they have received in their lives, but they use that power in a way that blesses and benefits others—as opposed to using it to point to their own abilities and lording their skills over everyone else.

Jesus is a perfect example of how God intends for you to use your power. He showed patience with His disciples when they missed the point. He gave credit to His heavenly Father for the miracles that He performed. He called out the hypocrisy of the religious elite. In one beautiful display, He defended a "sinful woman" who washed his feet with her tears (see Luke 7:36–50). Jesus could have scorned her and sent her away because of her sinful life. He could have also told the people who had gathered that this was the appropriate response for a woman who had run her life into the ground. Jesus did neither. Instead, He accepted her offering, commended the beauty in it, and forgave her sins.

Jesus, in spite of all the power He had been given, was also willing to take on the duties of a servant. At the Last Supper, Jesus washed the disciples' feet (see John 13:1–17). He was above them in every way, yet He knelt and performed a servant's job.

When Peter protested, Jesus explained that He was setting an example for them to model. As His followers, they were to remember that no servant is greater than his master. The church that Jesus was establishing, with the disciples as the foundation, would be built on humility and service to God.

In this final session, you will explore how the same is true for you today. God has placed His power *in* you so it will flow *out* to others. But the way that you are to demonstrate God's power in you is through acts of humble service. In this way, you follow the example that Jesus established.

OPENING PRAYER

Father, be with me as I face hard questions about how I am using the power that You have given me. Help me to have the humility to see where I have messed up. Give me the courage to make things right where I can, ask for forgiveness, and learn the lessons I need to learn. Amen.

BEGINNING QUESTION

To get things started, discuss one of these questions as a group:

- How do you tend to react when the power goes out in your home?

  — *or* —

- When is a time that God convicted you of pride? How did you respond to that conviction?

CONSIDER YOUR LIFE

Remember the assessment you took in the first session? You were asked to make a list of four areas in your life where you currently feel powerless and then envision how your life would change if you were to gain power in that area. Now it's time to check your progress. In the table below, write down any of the areas you previously listed where you have now *gained* power. In the next column, write down the changes and improvements you have *actually* witnessed as a result of taking the steps to gain power in those areas.

	Areas where you have gained power	What has actually changed for you
1		
2		
3		
4		

1. How closely does what you *envisioned* would happen if you gained power match up with what you *actually* experienced? Was anything better than you expected? Explain.

2. If there are any items on your original list where you still feel powerless, what is one small step you could take this week—based on everything you have learned in this study—that would move you closer to gaining power? Will you commit to taking that step?

DISCUSS AS A GROUP

Use the following questions to help you marinate on the main themes from chapters 16–18 of *Power Moves*, engage in discussion, and apply the concepts to your life. You've been consistent and faithful so far, so finish strong!

1. Read Acts 1:3–8. Jesus instructed His followers to remain in Jerusalem so they would receive power from the Holy Spirit. But Jesus never intended that power to just remain with them. What were they to do once they received the Holy Spirit's power?

2. Look up Matthew 20:25–28. Those who receive God's power have a responsibility in how they use it. What did Jesus say about the way in which the rulers and Gentiles exercised power? How was this different from the way His disciples were to use power?

3. What do you find surprising in Jesus' words about using power? Why is what He said so countercultural to the way that we see people using power today?

4. There is a relationship between power and humility. You cannot have one without the other and lead a healthy life. Who in your world displays this kind of proper balance between power and humility? What does that person do that especially stands out?

5. Read James 3:1–2. What warning does James provide in this passage about using your God-given authority? Why do you think those who teach are judged more strictly?

Do nothing out of selfish ambition or vain conceit. Rather, in humility value others above yourselves, not looking to your own interests but each of you to the interests of the others. In your relationships with one another, have the same mindset as Christ Jesus:

Who, being in very nature God,
        did not consider equality with God something
        to be used to his own advantage;
rather, he made himself nothing
        by taking the very nature of a servant,
        being made in human likeness.
And being found in appearance as a man,
        he humbled himself
        by becoming obedient to death—
                even death on a cross!
Therefore God exalted him to the highest place
        and gave him the name that is above
        every name,
that at the name of Jesus every knee should bow,
        in heaven and on earth and under the earth,
and every tongue acknowledge that Jesus
Christ is Lord,
        to the glory of God the Father.

PHILIPPIANS 2:3–11

6. Read the passage from Philippians 2:3–11 on the opposite page. Jesus had received all authority from God, but He never used this power to oppress others. How many times is *humility* mentioned in this passage? How many examples of Jesus' humility are shown?

7. Paul states that when it comes to your relationships with others, you are to "have the same mindset as Christ Jesus" (verse 5). What kind of mindset did Jesus have when it came to His relationships with people? What would it look like if you adopted that same kind of mindset? What would change and what would remain the same?

8. As you consider the topic of humility, what do you do with hard feedback when you receive it? How can introspection and prayer be a powerful tool in processing it?

" Blessed is the one
    whose transgressions are forgiven,
    whose sins are covered.
Blessed is the one
    whose sin the LORD does not count against them
    and in whose spirit is no deceit.

When I kept silent,
    my bones wasted away
    through my groaning all day long.
For day and night
    your hand was heavy on me;
my strength was sapped
    as in the heat of summer.

Then I acknowledged my sin to you
    and did not cover up my iniquity.
I said, "I will confess
    my transgressions to the LORD."
And you forgave
    the guilt of my sin.

Therefore let all the faithful pray to you
    while you may be found;
surely the rising of the mighty waters
    will not reach them.
You are my hiding place;
    you will protect me from trouble
    and surround me with songs of deliverance.

PSALM 32:1–7

9. Read the passage from Psalm 32:1–7 on the opposite page. There is nothing more powerful than being able to take accountability for where you've messed up so that you can move ahead and grow. What does the psalmist say happened when he refused to take accountability for his sins? Whom in this psalm does he say is "blessed"?

10. What are some of the repercussions you have witnessed in your own life of not admitting your mistakes and asking for forgiveness? Is there anyone you need to seek forgiveness from right now? If so, what will you do to make that happen?

APPLY WHAT YOU LEARNED

In this session, we have looked at how God wants to pour His power into us so that we can positively impact the lives of others. However, a huge part of being able to operate in God's power is *humility*. We have looked at several examples of how Jesus—our ultimate role model—accomplished this in His ministry. But let's look at one final example from the cross.

Jesus didn't have to endure the crucifixion. When the soldiers came to arrest Him, He told His disciples, "Do you think I cannot call on my Father, and he will at once put at my disposal more than twelve legions of angels?" (Matthew 26:53). He didn't have to endure the beatings that He was given, or the pain of having the nails driven into His flesh, or the mocking that He received from the onlookers. He had the power to make it all stop. But He didn't.

Instead, Jesus allowed power to move through Him. His last words from the cross were, "Father, into your hands I commit my spirit" (Luke 23:46). He completely surrendered to His Father, trusted the greater plan, and did not deviate from the course that the Father had set for Him. As one writer put it, "For the joy set before him he endured the cross" (Hebrews 12:2). Jesus gave up His life for us like a seed gives up its life when it goes into the ground. He died on the cross so there could be a multiplication of life.

When Jesus came out of that grave, no one could deny His power—and that power is still alive in us today. So let's use it well and for the glory of our God! It's time now to settle in one last time and allow God's Word to transform you. Sit with the following questions and apply them to your life so you can see the power of God at work in your life.

1. Jesus told a parable in Matthew 5:14–16 that reveals how God intends for His power to flow through us to impact others. What does Jesus say about light in this passage? What are we instructed to do with the power and light that God has placed within us?

2. Paul made a surprising claim that God's power "is made perfect in weakness" (2 Corinthians 12:9). Paul had a weakness that he called "a thorn" in his flesh (verse 7), but he had come to recognize he could

actually "boast all the more gladly" about it (verse 9) because God was using it to strengthen him. What kind of "thorn" like this do you have in your life? How can you boast in that particular weakness?

3. Paul stated, "God chose the weak things of the world to shame the strong" (1 Corinthians 1:27). How has God used your experiences of weakness to bring hope and life to someone else? Are you in a place where you can thank God for the circumstances and events that you have gone through? Why or why not?

4. *Fear* is a power-killer. Satan knows that if he can keep you afraid of moving forward, you will remain locked up from moving into the plans God has for you. Paul wrote, "The Spirit you received does not make you slaves, so that you live in fear again" (Romans 8:15). How are you allowing fear to keep you in bondage? How will you combat any spirit of fear in your life so you can move forward?

5. God said, "People look at the outward appearance, but the LORD looks at the heart" (1 Samuel 16:7). This verse reveals how people will receive the way you show up in the world. What happens when your outward presentation doesn't match what is in your heart to see God's power move in radical ways? What does this say about the need for authenticity in all of your relationships?

PRAY TO CLOSE

Father, thank You for teaching me how Your power is alive and active in my life. You are my source of power, and I am grateful that You guide me every step of the way. Help me to take ownership of things I can do better. Help me to be humble in the areas where You have blessed me. I give my words, thoughts, and actions to You. Use me, Lord. I am willing. Amen.

Leader's Guide

Thank you for your willingness to lead your group through this study! What you have chosen to do is valuable and will make a great difference in the lives of others. The *Power Moves Bible Study Guide* is a six-session study built around the book content and small-group interaction. As the group leader, imagine yourself as the host of a party. Your job is to take care of your guests by managing the details so that when your guests arrive, they can focus on the interaction around the topic for that session.

Your role as the group leader is not to answer all the questions or reteach the content—this guide will do most of that work. Your job is to guide the experience and cultivate your small group into a connected and engaged community. This will make it a place for members to process, question, and reflect—not necessarily receive more instruction. There are several elements in this leader's guide that will help you as you structure your study and reflection time, so be sure to follow along and take advantage of each one.

BEFORE YOU BEGIN

Before your first meeting, make sure the members have a copy of this Bible study guide. Alternatively, you can hand them out at your first meeting and give the members some time to look over the material and ask any preliminary questions. During your first meeting, ask the members to provide their name, phone number, and email address so you can keep in touch during the week.

Generally, the ideal size for a small group is eight to ten people, which will ensure that everyone has enough time to participate in discussions. If you have more people, you might want to break up the main group into smaller subgroups. Encourage those who show up at the first meeting to commit to attending the duration of the study, as this will help the group members get to know one another, create stability for the group, and help you know how to best prepare to lead them through the material.

LEADING THE GROUP TIME

Each session begins with a reflection that either the group members can read on their own or you can read out loud. An opening prayer has also been provided to help you get things started—but feel free to pray for the group members in any way that you feel led by the Lord. The questions that follow serve as an icebreaker to get the group members thinking about the topic. Some people may want to tell a long story in response to one of these questions, but the goal is to keep the answers brief. Ideally, you want everyone in the group to get a chance to answer, so try to keep the responses to a minute or less. If you have talkative group members, say up front that everyone needs to limit their answer to one minute.

Give the group members a chance to answer, but also tell them to feel free to pass if they wish. With the rest of the study, it's generally not a good idea to have everyone answer every question—a free-flowing discussion is more desirable. But with the opening icebreaker questions, you can go around the circle. Encourage shy people to share, but don't force them.

Following the icebreaker question, give the group members a few minutes (no more than five to ten) to complete the "Consider Your Life" exercise. You can then go through each of the discussion questions, looking up the passages of Scripture as directed. After your time of discussion, allow a few more minutes for the group to go through the "Apply What You Learned" activity to cement the key concepts of the session in their minds. Close with prayer.

PREPARATION FOR EACH SESSION

As the leader, there are a few things that you should do to prepare for each meeting:

- **Read through the session.** This will help you become more familiar with the content and know how to structure the discussion time.

- **Decide which questions you want to discuss.** Based on the length of your group discussions, you may not be able to get through all of the questions. So, ahead of time, choose which ones you definitely want to cover.

- **Be familiar with the questions you want to discuss.** When the group meets, you will be watching the clock, so make sure that you are familiar with each of the questions that you have selected. In this way, you will ensure that you have the material more deeply in your mind than your group members.

- **Pray for your group.** Continue to pray for your group members during the week and ask God to lead them as they study His Word.

Note that in many cases, there will not be a "right" answer to the discussion questions. Answers will vary, especially when group members are sharing their personal experiences.

GROUP DYNAMICS

Leading a group through *Power Moves* will prove to be highly rewarding both to you and your group members. But you still may encounter challenges along the way! Discussions can get off track. Group members may not be sensitive to the needs and ideas of others. Some might worry they will be expected to talk about matters that make them feel awkward. Others may express comments that result in disagreements. To help ease this strain on you and the group, consider the following ground rules:

- When someone raises a question or comment that is off the main topic, suggest that you deal with it another time, or, if you feel led to go in that direction, let the group know you will be spending some time discussing it.

- If someone asks a question that you don't know how to answer, admit it and move on. At your discretion, feel free to invite group members to comment on questions that call for personal experience.

- If you find one or two people are dominating the discussion time, direct a few questions to others in the group. Outside the main group time, ask the more dominating members to help you draw out the quieter ones. Work to make them a part of the solution instead of part of the problem.

- When a disagreement occurs, encourage the group members to process the matter in love. Encourage those on opposite sides to restate what they heard the other side say about the matter, and then invite each side to evaluate if that perception is accurate. Lead the group in examining other scriptures related to the topic, and look for common ground.

When any of these issues arise—or any others not mentioned here—encourage your group members to "love one another" (John 13:34), "live at peace with everyone" (Romans 12:18), and "be quick to listen, slow to speak and slow to become angry" (James 1:19). This will make your group time more rewarding and beneficial for everyone who attends.

Thank you again for leading your group! You are making a difference in your group members' lives and having an impact on how they understand the power of God within them.

Scriptures FOR
FURTHER REFLECTION

The following are additional verses and passages of Scripture related to the topics presented in each session of this study guide. Consider looking these up in the weeks ahead and write them down. You can take them into your quiet time with the Lord and ask what He wants to say to you through them. You might even want to post them around your house so you can see them often and be continually reminded of the *power* you have in Christ.

SESSION 1: POWER THROUGH CONNECTION
Psalm 25:14
Psalm 145:18
Matthew 7:7
John 15:15
1 John 1:3
1 John 3:24

SESSION 2: POWER TO GET UNSTUCK
Psalm 51:10–12
Matthew 6:33
Mark 9:23
2 Corinthians 3:18
2 Corinthians 5:17
Galatians 2:20

SESSION 3: POWER TO BE USED BY GOD
Joshua 1:9
Isaiah 41:9–10
Jeremiah 29:11
Ephesians 1:11–12
Ephesians 2:10
2 Timothy 1:9–10

SESSION 4: POWER TO ENGAGE IN BATTLE
Psalm 91:9–10
Luke 10:19
1 Corinthians 1:10
2 Corinthians 10:3–5
James 4:7
1 John 5:3–5

SESSION 5: POWER TO SEE GOD MOVE
Psalm 119:18
Matthew 13:10–12
Luke 24:44–45
John 14:12
John 14:26
John 16:13

SESSION 6: POWER TO CHANGE LIVES
Acts 20:35
Colossians 3:16
Colossians 3:23–24
1 Thessalonians 5:11
2 Timothy 2:2
1 Peter 4:10

NOTES

1. *Oxford English Dictionary*, s.v. "power," https://oed.com/search/dictionary/?scope=Entries&q=power.
2. *Collins English Dictionary*, s.v. "staying power," https://collinsdictionary.com/us/dictionary/english/staying-power.
3. *Merriam-Webster*, s.v. "staying power," https://merriam-webster.com/dictionary/stayingpower.
4. Sarah Jakes Roberts, *Power Moves* (Nashville, TN: W Publishing Group, 2024), 7–8.
5. Roberts, *Power Moves*, 61–62.
6. *Merriam-Webster*, s.v. "stick," https://www.merriam-webster.com/dictionary/stick.
7. *Merriam-Webster*, s.v. "pattern," https://www.merriam-webster.com/dictionary/pattern.
8. Roberts, *Power Moves*, 84.
9. Oswald Chambers, "The Source of Abundant Joy," *My Utmost for His Highest*, entry for March 7, https://utmost.org/the-source-of-abundant-joy/.
10. Roberts, *Power Moves*, 110.
11. Roberts, *Power Moves*, 142–143.
12. "The Gestalt Principles," Interaction Design Foundation, https://www.interaction-design.org/literature/topics/gestalt-principles.
13. "Pareidolia," *Psychology Today*, https://www.psychologytoday.com/us/basics/pareidolia.
14. Roberts, *Power Moves*, 185.

ABOUT
Sarah Jakes Roberts

Sarah Jakes Roberts is an author, speaker, entrepreneur, and philan-thropist. She is the founder of Woman Evolve, a multimedia plat-form that provides women with the tools, support, and encouragement necessary to make positive and lasting changes. Through various resources such as digital and live events, books, podcasts, and online content, Woman Evolve seeks to address the holistic needs of women and empower them to lead fulfilling and impactful lives.

Alongside her husband, Touré Roberts, Sarah copastors at ONE Los Angeles and serves in leadership at The Potter's House Dallas. Her messages are spread throughout the world, defying cultural, religious, gender, and socioeconomic boundaries. With her down-to-earth personality, contemporary style, and revelatory messages, there's no question why Time100 Next named her an emerging thought leader for this generation.